C000225436

# *from*
# *to the Kennet*

Compiled by
Nick Channer

publishing

Mapping
sourced from
Ordnance
Survey®

| Text: | Nick Channer |
|---|---|
| **Photography:** | Nick Channer |
| **Editor:** | Crawford Gillan |
| **Designer:** | Sarah Crouch |

© Jarrold Publishing 2004

 This product includes mapping data licensed from Ordnance Survey® with the permission of the Controller of Her Majesty's Stationery Office. © Crown Copyright 2003. All rights reserved. Licence number 100017593. Ordnance Survey, the OS symbol and Pathfinder are registered trademarks and Explorer, Landranger and Outdoor Leisure are trademarks of the Ordnance Survey, the national mapping agency of Great Britain.

Jarrold Publishing
ISBN 0-7117-3002-4

First published 2004
by Jarrold Publishing

Printed in Belgium
by Proost NV, Turnhout. 1/04

**Jarrold Publishing**
Pathfinder Guides, Whitefriars,
Norwich NR3 1JR
E-mail: info@totalwalking.co.uk
www.totalwalking.co.uk

**Front cover:** Avebury cottages and view from the Giant's Grave
**Previous page:** Avebury Stone Circle

# Contents

# Keymap

SCALE 1:384 615 or 1 INCH to about 6 MILES *1CM to 3.8KM*

0  2  4  6  8  10 KILOMETRES  15

0  2  4  6 MILES 8  10

**KEYMAP HEIGHTS SHOWN IN FEET**

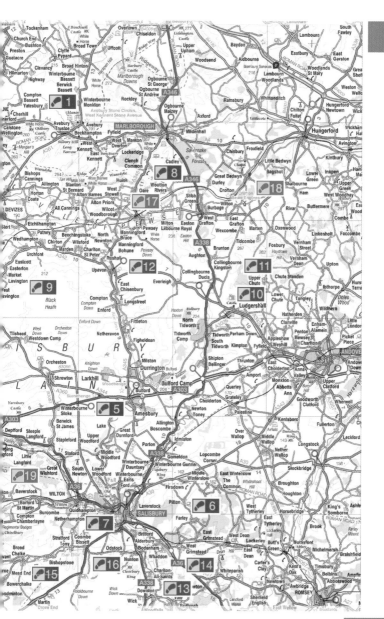

# Introduction

The routes and information in this book have been devised specifically with families and children in mind. All the walks include points of interest as well as a question to provide an objective.

If you, or your children, have not walked before, choose from the shorter walks for your first outings, although none of the walks is especially demanding. The purpose is not simply to get from A to B, but to enjoy an exploration, which may be just a steady stroll in the countryside, alongside rivers, lakes and expansive plain, through woodlands or climbing hills.

The walks are graded by length and difficulty, but few landscapes are truly flat, so even short walks may involve some ascent. Details are given under Route Features in the first information box for each route, but the precise nature of the ground underfoot will depend on recent weather conditions. If you do set out on a walk and discover the going is harder than you expected, or the weather has deteriorated, do not be afraid to turn back. The route will always be there another day, when you are fitter or the children are more experienced or the weather is better.

*Nunton church*

*Castle Combe*

Bear in mind that the countryside also changes. Landmarks may disappear, gates may become stiles and rights of way may be altered. However, with the aid of this book and its maps you should be able to enjoy many interesting family walks in the countryside.

## Wiltshire – from Salisbury to the Kennet

Thankfully, Wiltshire remains an unspoiled corner of England. At its heart lie some of the wildest and least populated landscapes in the country, littered with timeless prehistoric sites, monoliths and barrows. You don't have to travel far before stumbling upon clear evidence of early human habitation. Various rivers and canals cross Wiltshire and over the years they, too, have played an important part in shaping the county's varied and ancient history. The walks in this book are mainly concentrated in an area of Wiltshire bounded by the River Kennet, a tributary of the Thames, to the north and the beautiful cathedral city of Salisbury and the rivers Ebble and Nadder to the south. The routes are designed to take advantage of the county's glorious mix of picturesque villages, dramatic sweeps of chalk downland and tranquil river valley scenery.

## Avebury

To the north lies the ancient settlement of Avebury, renowned for its antiquities. Up to 500,000 visitors a year descend on this village, inspecting and photographing the legendary stone circle that has stood on this site since Neolithic times. Avebury, which may be a burial ground for tribal chiefs, was drastically altered by the archaeologist and marmalade heir Alexander Keiller who acquired the site in the mid 1930s. What we see today is largely his creation. He demolished cottages, felled trees and removed fences. His main aim was to remove any sign of human habitation from within the stone circle, a policy later adopted by the National Trust, Avebury's owner.

## The Kennet and Avon and the Marlborough Downs

Nearby lies the Kennet and Avon Canal, running east to west across Wiltshire and serving as a lasting monument to the engineering achievements of the pre-railway era. After extensive restoration work, the canal reopened in 1990 and today you can follow it for more than 80 miles (128km) on foot or by boat between Reading and Bristol. A stone's throw from the Wiltshire section of the canal

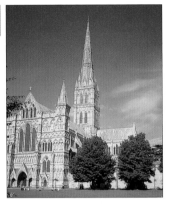
*Salisbury Cathedral*

are the wonderfully invigorating and breezy Marlborough Downs, once one of the most populated areas in the country, inhabited by the people of the late Stone Age and Bronze Age. This is where spectacular scarp scenery gives way to the low-lying clay country of the Vale of Pewsey.

## Salisbury Plain

To the south of the vale lies the Stone Age landscape of Salisbury Plain, now used as a military training area. Not surprisingly, most of this enigmatic 300 square-mile tract of land is off limits to walkers. However, the scenic Wessex Ridgeway and the Imber Range Path skirt these lonely and eerily silent tracts of open country, providing magnificent views across Salisbury Plain to distant horizons.

## New Sarum and its historic cathedral

In the south-east corner of Wiltshire stands the beautiful city of Salisbury, perfect for exploring on foot. The site of the magnificent cathedral was chosen when Bishop Richard Poore abandoned the Norman cathedral on the fortified hill of Old Sarum because it lacked a proper and efficient water supply. The lush meadows on the lower ground were thought to be more suitable and the alternative site was called 'New Sarum'. Around every corner and along every street in this very English city is something new and surprising. You can spend all day here, savouring Salisbury's rarefied atmosphere and visiting its many attractions.

## Wiltshire's Rivers

The county's streams and rivers are some of the finest in the country and nowhere is this better illustrated than along Wiltshire's southern boundary. Here, you will find the crystal waters of the Wylye, the Nadder and the Ebble – among others – meandering peacefully through their chalk valleys. Numerous paths and tracks flirt with these waterways, crossing and recrossing them and running alongside them.

## Long-distance walks

Some of the walks in this guide coincide with stretches of long-distance paths. The Monarch's Way is a fascinating trail which follows Charles II's escape route after the Battle of Worcester in 1651. For six weeks, avidly pursued by Parliamentary forces under Oliver Cromwell, Charles travelled first north, then south through the Cotswold hills and the Mendips to the South Coast, where he fled to France. The 85-mile (136km) Ridgeway National Trail, extending between Ivinghoe Beacon in Buckinghamshire and Avebury, follows Britain's oldest road, an important trade route. Wiltshire is a walker's paradise – whether you want long-distance trails or short strolls. A land steeped in ancient history, myth and legend, it captures the best of Britain's varied scenery. Sparsely populated with communities scattered across an often desolate landscape, the county conveys a strong sense of space, solitude and distance.

*The Kennet and Avon at Pewsey Wharf*

# 1 *Around Avebury's ancient stones*

**START** Avebury
**DISTANCE** 3 miles (4.8km)
**TIME** 1½ hours
**PARKING** Free car park in the High Street
**ROUTE FEATURES** Field and riverside paths, optional spur to West Kennett Long Barrow

*The picturesque village of Avebury is widely acknowledged as one of the country's most popular visitor attractions and is famous throughout the world for its ancient standing stones. Starting in the shadow of the stones, the walk soon leaves the village, cutting across a primitive, windswept landscape to reach the pretty River Kennet near its source.*

From the car park turn left to the Red Lion and cross the main road to the gate. Walk ahead between the stones and when the path curves gently by some beech trees, keep right and follow the fence with the road to the right of it. Go through the trees to a gate, cross the road to another gate and follow the path alongside the Stone Avenue (B4003), a grassy path running parallel to the road Ⓐ.

Walk down to a gate, cross into the next field via two gates and still keep the road on the left. Look for a stile leading out to the B4003, turn right and follow the road down to the A4. Turn right, then take the first left turning Ⓑ.

Charles II was recommended by John Aubrey to visit Avebury in 1663 because '...it does as much exceed in greatness the renowned Stonehenge as a Cathedral doeth a parish church...' Consisting of a substantial outer bank and inner ditch, **Avebury** is regarded by historians as one of Europe's most important Neolithic sites. The brooding standing stones make up one of the largest remaining henge monuments, even older than Stonehenge.

**PUBLIC TRANSPORT** Bus service from Swindon, Salisbury, Calne, Devizes and Trowbridge
**REFRESHMENTS** A pub and a café in Avebury
**PUBLIC TOILETS** Avebury
**ORDNANCE SURVEY MAPS** Explorer 157 (Marlborough & Savernake Forest) and Landranger 173 (Swindon & Devizes)

Cross the River Kennet and turn right to join a track. Along here the familiar outline of Silbury Hill edges into view. Make for a gate and stile and keep ahead, with the field boundary on your right. On reaching a path junction, you have a choice **C**.

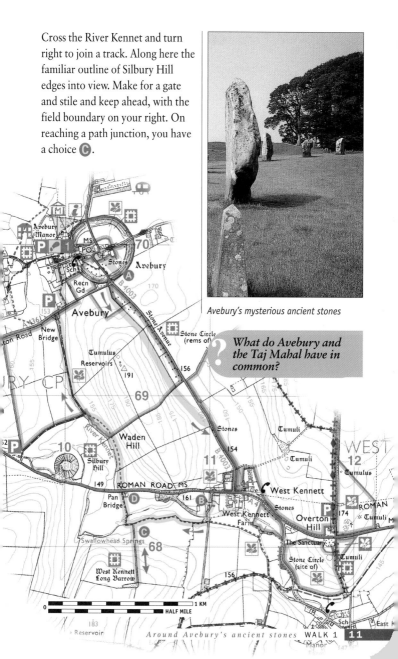

*Avebury's mysterious ancient stones*

**What do Avebury and the Taj Mahal have in common?**

*Silbury Hill – the largest man-made mound in prehistoric Europe*

*To extend the walk, turn left to visit the West Kennett Long Barrow, one of the longest burial mounds in England and Wales. The barrow was built around 3,500 BC and was eventually sealed 1,000 years later. During this time 40 to 50 people were buried here.* To continue the walk turn right, recross the Kennet and make for the A4 **D**.

Cross over to a gate and path signposted Avebury. Keep the river and Silbury Hill on your left, cross two stiles, pass a river crossing and follow the path all the way to the A4361. Cross over to Avebury car park, join the path here and walk along to the village centre. Turn right and return to the High Street car park.  ●

You can't fail to spot another **legendary landmark** on the walk's return leg. Constructed 4,600 years ago, Silbury Hill is the largest man-made mound in prehistoric Europe. Built on a spur of natural chalk, this huge engineering project involved millions of hours of labour, though its precise age is still a mystery.

# Castle Combe and a fantasy film set

**START** Castle Combe

**DISTANCE** 3 miles (4.8km)

**TIME** 1½ hours

**PARKING** Free car park just outside Castle Combe

**ROUTE FEATURES** Pretty undulating landscape, pleasant sections by the By Brook. Some moderate climbing, wet in woodland after heavy rain

**2**

*Set in a secluded wooded hollow, Castle Combe is one of Britain's most visited sites. Looking at its quaint streets and picturesque stone houses, it is easy to see why. Starting from the village, the walk is equally delightful, exploring tranquil valleys and tumbling wooded hillsides to the south of Castle Combe. In places, the route runs alongside the By Brook, a tributary of the Avon.*

🖋 Take a leisurely stroll through Castle Combe, looking at the church and the various attractions and then follow the street down to the By Brook. Cross it and take the road out of the village, heading for a footpath and three steps on the right **A**.

Climb diagonally up the bank under the branches of beech trees and keep ahead at the top, following the waymark. Walk along to the road and turn left, avoiding another path on the left. Continue down to the junction and go straight on for a few paces towards Ford.

**B** Turn right to join a path, then swing immediately left, following the path parallel to the road (signposted Ford). The ground falls away dramatically to the right as you cut through the trees. Make for a stile and continue ahead

**PUBLIC TRANSPORT** Bus services from Chippenham

**REFRESHMENTS** The White Hart and the Castle Inn, Castle Combe, and the White Hart at Ford

**PUBLIC TOILETS** Castle Combe

**ORDNANCE SURVEY MAPS** Explorer 156 (Chippenham & Bradford-on-Avon) and Landranger 173 (Swindon & Devizes)

across open ground and rather lumpy terrain. Wild flowers can be seen on this stretch in summer. Pass a waymark and descend steeply through trees to reach a stone bridge and a wooden footbridge.

The 'castle' which gives the village its name was originally a **Roman fort** and was occupied by the Saxons before becoming a Norman Castle in 1135. Later Castle Combe became an important weaving community, with fulling mills erected along the By Brook. Its wealth and prosperity grew to such an extent that it eventually became a town with a weekly market and an annual fair.

**C** Keep ahead and follow the path as it runs through woodland above a stream. Cross a pasture, keeping to the right of a house, and go down to a stile by its entrance. Walk down the drive into the village of Ford. To the right is the church, its churchyard managed as a conservation area. The lighting and two heaters were given by the mother of a young man killed on active service in 1944. The White Hart is nearby on the Colerne road.

**D** Turn left and walk along the A420 to a turning for Castle Combe. Follow the lane uphill through the trees to a sign for the Macmillan Way and stride out across the field, keeping

*Castle Combe – a popular film and television location*

to the path as it curves gently round the hillside in line with the contours. Go through a galvanised gate and follow a shaded, sunken path. Join a track running through the hamlet of Long Dean and turn left at a staggered junction by a postbox.

Ⓔ Make for two gates and stiles and looking down through the trees on the left you can see the By Brook. At length you reach a fork. Keep left here and follow the lower path to a stile. Continue to an old stone bridge, cross over to the road and turn right. Return to Castle Combe. ●

**?** *What type of fish are you likely to see in the By Brook at Castle Combe?*

You might recognise Castle Combe even if you have never been here before. The village was used as a film location for the 1967 version of Hugh Lofting's timeless children's classic **Doctor Doolittle**, starring Rex Harrison, Anthony Newley and Richard Attenborough. A jetty was built by the cottages overlooking the By Brook to create a fishing harbour and villagers were employed as extras at £2.50 a day. An episode of Agatha Christie's **Poirot** was filmed at Castle Combe in 1999.

# 3 Bradford-on-Avon

**START** Bradford-on-Avon
**DISTANCE** 3 miles (4.8km)
**TIME** 1½ hours
**PARKING** Fee-paying car parks in Bradford-on-Avon
**ROUTE FEATURES** Historic tithe barn, canal towpath, aqueduct, riverside path and town trail to Saxon church. Gentle climbing

*Water is very much the theme on this varied walk which is both a country ramble and a town trail. Initially, the route follows the Kennet and Avon Canal before climbing above this most popular of inland waterways to cut through silent woodland, wonderfully cool on a hot day. From the impressive Avoncliff Aqueduct, the walk follows the Avon back into Bradford, visiting the ancient Saxon church of St Laurence en route.*

Walk to the far end of the station car park, pass under the railway line and follow the path along to the 14th century tithe barn, noted for its splendid roof structure. On a sunny day, it is pleasantly dark and cool inside.

Ⓐ On leaving the barn, turn left and follow the path up some steps to the Kennet and Avon Canal. Turn right and follow the towpath. Cross over at the footbridge (173),

*Bradford-on-Avon's Saxon church*

**PUBLIC TRANSPORT** Bus services to Bath, Trowbridge, Warminster and Salisbury. Train services to Bath, Trowbridge, Westbury and Salisbury
**REFRESHMENTS** Pubs and cafés in Bradford-on-Avon and at the Avoncliff Aqueduct
**PUBLIC TOILETS** Bradford-on-Avon
**ORDNANCE SURVEY MAPS** Explorer 156 (Chippenham & Bradford-on-Avon) and Landranger 173 (Swindon & Devizes)

built in 1992, and keep right. With the canal on your right, cross a footbridge and stile and skirt the field. Make for the next stile and head diagonally up the field slope. **B** Look back when you reach the top and you get a memorable view of Bradford-on-Avon. Go through a wrought-iron kissing-gate and follow the woodland path. Farther on it widens before climbing to reach the road.

Turn right and descend through the trees. Pass one of the entrances to Ancliff Square and a footpath on the left. **C** Emerging from the woodland, Avoncliff Aqueduct is seen ahead now, with the Mad Hatter Tearoom on the left. Keep it on your left and go down to some steps on the right. Pass under the aqueduct to reach the 17th century Cross Guns pub.

One of Bradford-on-Avon's most historic landmarks is the Saxon church of **St Laurence** which dates from about AD 700. Tall and narrow with small windows, it was abandoned for centuries until Canon Jones, a noted historian, rediscovered it in 1856 and recognised it as a late Saxon building. Look out for the carved angels high up on the east wall of the nave.

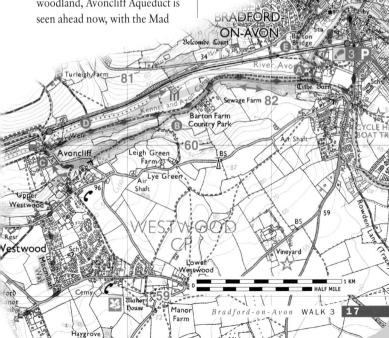

Walk back towards the Avoncliff Aqueduct, built in 1798 and 110 yds (100m) long, and make for the Kennet and Avon Canal towpath. Turn left and follow the path round a left bend. ⒹAfter a few paces you reach a map and canal information board. Veer left here and descend some steps. With a view of the weir on the left, turn right and follow the path through undergrowth, lush vegetation and meadows. The sound of trains is clearly audible.

Cut through the meadows of Barton Country Park and follow the path to the tithe barn. Turn left just beyond it and cross the packhorse bridge. Keep ahead to the railway line, cross over and follow the tarmac path as it curves right. ⒺWalk between sturdy

**Bradford-on-Avon**, meaning 'broad ford', is one of Wiltshire's loveliest towns. You can see at a glance it is hilly. Rows of elegant terraced houses and an assortment of ancient stone weavers' cottages rise dramatically above the main river bridge. For 600 years Bradford played a key role in the manufacture of wool and cloth and this tradition only ended at the start of the 20th century.

stone walls and picturesque houses and follow the signs for the Saxon church. Cross the footbridge beyond it, go through the car park to the road, turn right and right again for the station car park. ●

? *The packhorse bridge on the approach to the Saxon church is one of how many in the country?*

*Avoncliff Aqueduct*

# Bratton Camp and Westbury White Horse

**START** Bratton

**DISTANCE** 3 miles (4.8km)

**TIME** 1¾ hours

**PARKING** Free car park in Tynings Lane, Bratton

**ROUTE FEATURES** Initial climb on road, dramatic walk along camp ramparts to White Horse, scenic section of the Wessex Ridgeway and the Imber Range Path

**4**

*Far-reaching views and reminders of Wiltshire's distant past are the highlights on this spectacular walk. Very quickly the walk climbs to an ancient hillfort known as Bratton Camp before an exhilarating stroll along the site's surviving ramparts brings you to the much-loved Westbury White Horse. On the return leg savour the stillness and solitude of Salisbury Plain.*

From the car park walk along Tynings Lane, passing the Church Institute building. The stone for it was laid by the Marquess of Bath in 1910. Keep left at the T-junction and walk along to Castle Road.

Ⓐ Swing left here and begin a moderate climb. Farther up, a bridleway crosses the road. Disregard it and continue ascending, the road becoming noticeably steeper now. When the lane curves left, veer half right to join a track by Bratton Camp. Keep to the right of the site, following a clear path across the top of the ramparts.

Wiltshire's **oldest white horse** is 180ft (55m) long and 108ft (33m) high. Dating back to 1778 and thought to replace a much earlier figure cut in celebration of King Alfred's victory over the Danes in AD 878, the White Horse is best seen from a distance. Next to it is **Bratton Camp**, an Iron Age hillfort covering 25 acres (10ha) including a long barrow burial mound probably built before 3000 BC.

**PUBLIC TRANSPORT** Bus services between Trowbridge, Westbury and Devizes

**REFRESHMENTS** The Duke pub in Bratton

**ORDNANCE SURVEY MAPS** Explorer 143 (Warminster & Trowbridge) and Landranger 184 (Salisbury & The Plain)

**B** Walk along to the White Horse and look for a flight of steps immediately above the horse's head. These provide access to the fort. Keep to the right of the long barrow and once again walk along the top of the ramparts. A car park is seen over to the right. As you approach a lane, veer right down over the ditches to a stile. On reaching the access road to the car park, swing left to the T-junction.

**C** Turn right towards a mast and some trees and walk along to the buildings of White Horse Farm. Ahead lies the vast expanse of Salisbury Plain – empty, abandoned and rather sinister. Turn left here and follow the Wessex Ridgeway. Pass a track with a 'keep out' sign on the right and walk along to a gated bridleway on the left.

**D** Follow the track to three gates. Go through the middle gate and continue on the bridleway as it bends left and then right. Remain on the sunken track and ahead is a stunning view of west Wiltshire. Make for a gate and swing right immediately before it. Keep the fence on the left, go through a gate with a bridleway waymark and follow the field boundary. The tower of Bratton church can be seen down below.

*Bratton's 13th-century church at the base of chalk downland*

**E** When you reach an arrow on a fence post, head diagonally down the escarpment towards the church. At length pass through some trees and cross the pasture to a stile in the left corner. Go down some steps, avoid a second stile on the right and follow the path alongside the churchyard. Go down and then up a flight of steps, cross a lane and continue on the path to the next road. Turn right and return to the centre of Bratton. ●

**? What do you notice about the Westbury White Horse?**

*Westbury White Horse on the downs near Bratton*

Bratton's **Church of St James the Great** is one of the county's finest buildings. It looks magnificent, standing among the trees and set against a dramatic downland backdrop. The architecture is very striking – the embattled 15th century tower has grinning gargoyles and a stair turret, the arcades rest on clustered columns and the north transept has angels playing musical instruments or carrying shields.

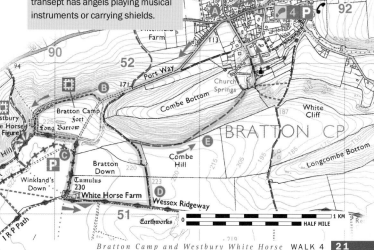

*Bratton Camp and Westbury White Horse* WALK 4 **21**

# 5 Amesbury and along the River Avon

**START** Amesbury
**DISTANCE** 2½ miles (4km)
**TIME** 1½ hours
**PARKING** Amesbury – Church Street car park. Maximum stay Monday to Saturday 3 hours
**ROUTE FEATURES** Pleasant walking by the River Avon followed by a stretch of dramatic downland. Gentle climbing

*Amesbury is the perfect starting point for an exhilarating Wiltshire walk. Just a stone's throw from this bustling little town lies a fine mixture of rural scenery explored on this easy stroll. From the church the walk makes for the banks of the River Avon and then crosses breezy, uncluttered country. Not far away is the world-famous site of Stonehenge.*

 Turn right out of the car park by the Antrobus Arms Hotel, passing the Old Vicarage and the Church of St Mary and St Melor. On the left is the Royal British Legion. Walk along to the five-span stone bridge crossing the Avon and, when the road bends right, turn left by a thatched cottage called Little Thatch.

Ⓐ Go through a kissing-gate and follow the sign for South Mill. There are good views of Amesbury across the pasture. Pass the entrance to a sewage treatment works and continue ahead on a rough track leading to a gateway. Don't go through it. Instead, keep left of it and follow the path along the field edge. Pass some willow trees, go through a second kissing-gate and over several footbridges at South Mill.

> **?** *Where are you likely to see the date 1775 in Roman numerals?*

**PUBLIC TRANSPORT** Bus services from Swindon, Salisbury and Marlborough
**REFRESHMENTS** Pubs and cafés in Amesbury
**PUBLIC TOILETS** Amesbury
**ORDNANCE SURVEY MAPS** Explorer 130 (Salisbury & Stonehenge) and Landranger 184 (Salisbury & The Plain)

**B** Turn right at the road and follow the bridleway as it runs through trees beside the Avon. At any time of the year this is a delightful stretch. The river is a popular haunt of ducks. When the track forks, keep left and go up the slope, beginning a moderate climb. Merge with another track farther up and continue ahead.

**C** When you reach a junction of paths and tracks, turn right for Amesbury. This is a windswept, exposed section of the walk and can be very cold on a frosty winter's day. Follow the track down

between fields and pass a pair of semi-detached houses on the right.

**Amesbury Abbey**, rebuilt in the 19th century and now a nursing home, stands on the site of the original abbey which was constructed in AD 979. The present house was built by Thomas Hopper for Sir Edward Antrobus, owner of the Stonehenge estate. The Avon flows prettily through the parkland. Nearby is Amesbury's ancient church, built by the Saxons and remodelled by the Normans. However, the church you see today is essentially 13th century. It contains one rather unusual feature – a head carved into the aisle roof depicting Henry VIII as a cherub.

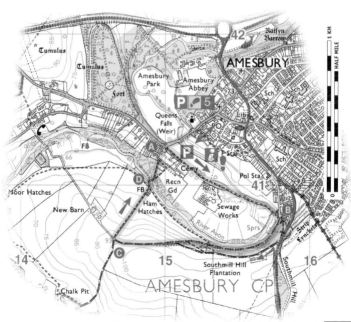

**D** Walk ahead into the wood and follow the riverside path to a bridge. Cross two more footbridges before reaching the recreation ground which lies to the right of the path. Follow it beside the entrance to a house called Abbots End. Pass the entrance to Amesbury Cemetery on the right and continue down to the road. Keep right and return to the centre of Amesbury. ●

Amesbury lies along the eastern edge of Salisbury Plain and is renowned for its Arthurian connections. Allegedly, **King Arthur** may have harboured a fondness for the area and there are also claims that the name 'Amesbury' comes from Ambrosius Aurelianus, a Roman Briton who happened to be the uncle of King Arthur. After the King's death in the 6th century, it is said that **Queen Guinevere** sought refuge in the Wessex region, probably fleeing to an abbey.

*The River Avon near Amesbury*

# Pitton and Church Copse

**START** Pitton
**DISTANCE** 2½ miles (4km)
**TIME** 1½ hours
**PARKING** Room to park in High Street, in the vicinity of the church and post office
**ROUTE FEATURES** Field paths and tracks, extensive woodland. Steep climb near the start

*You really feel as if you are stepping back into the distant past on this attractive woodland and farmland walk in a glorious fold of the South Wiltshire Downs. Farm labourers and foresters trudged along the local paths and tracks to earn their living and close by are the remains of a royal palace which began life as a Saxon hunting lodge.*

From St Peter's Church cross the road and take the path by the bus stop. Follow it alongside trees, fencing and hedgerow and on the left are several brick and timber barns. Pass the village recreation ground to reach the next road.

Ⓐ Cross it and take the path up the bank and through the trees, climbing steeply here between fencing, hedging and rough pasture. From the high ground there are stunning views over Pitton and the surrounding downland. The church is also visible among the trees. Cross two stiles and continue with a field boundary on the right.

*Church Copse*

**PUBLIC TRANSPORT** Bus services between Salisbury, Andover and Stockbridge
**REFRESHMENTS** Pub in Pitton
**ORDNANCE SURVEY MAPS** Explorer 131 (Romsey, Andover & Test Valley) and Landranger 184 (Salisbury & The Plain)

**B** Make for a track leading to Hale Farm, cross it and maintain the same direction, following the track alongside trees and bushes. Pass under the boughs of oak trees and approach a curtain of woodland. The track narrows to a path farther on and runs alongside trees, bushes and light woodland.

**C** Cross a stile and follow the obvious path as it veers to the right through the silent wood. The towering firs here create a cathedral-like canopy. At length the path joins a clear track. On the left is Church Copse. Keep right here,

> **St Peter's Church** at Pitton is even older than Salisbury Cathedral, dating back to the 12th century, though almost nothing remains of the original building. The present church was heavily restored in the late 1880s and the exterior was rendered with a flint and greensand dressing. Inside are an octagonal oak pulpit and a memorial brass plaque of 1580 commemorating the Zouche family who owned Pitton at the time of Charles I. St Peter's is Grade II listed.

pass a turning on the right followed by one on the left. Make for a major junction of rights-of-way and turn right over the stile. Avoid the path running diagonally across the field and keep the wood on your right.

> **?** *What is the silver farming implement seen in Pitton?*

*Picturesque Pitton*

**D** Skirt the woodland to reach a stile and follow a sometimes overgrown path for about 40 yds (36m) to a second stile. Keep ahead, inside the woodland now, and cut through the trees. Pass directly beneath telegraph wires and, on reaching a field, keep ahead with hedge boundary on the left. Cross into the next field and head diagonally right to reach the hedge corner. On reaching it, skirt the field with the boundary on your left.

**E** Make for a farm track, turn left and pass Pitton Hill Farm. Walk along to the road, turn right and note the distinctive chalk cliff on the right. Descend the hill into Pitton, pass the village sign and the 19th century Methodist chapel and head down to the main junction. Turn right into High Street. ●

**The Clarendon Way**, an old Saxon route linking Winchester with Old Sarum, runs through Pitton, providing glimpses of ancient woodland and giving a fascinating insight into rural life in the days when kings and their court hunted in the forest and great palaces and country houses dotted the countryside. The woods near Pitton yielded timber for the village's waggon-building and wheelwright businesses.

# 7 Salisbury – a heritage trail

*A stroll through the streets of Salisbury, one of Britain's loveliest cities, offers an assortment of riches. Firstly, there is the soaring spire of the cathedral, the tallest in England and immortalised by Constable in his famous painting. Towards the end of the heritage trail is Malmesbury House which Handel used for his recitals and where Charles II stayed at the time of the Great Plague.*

**START** Salisbury
**DISTANCE** 2 miles (32.km)
**TIME** 1 hour minimum
**PARKING** Plenty of car parks in Salisbury, mostly fee-paying
**ROUTE FEATURES** Salisbury Cathedral, gardens, riverside walking and a choice of museums. Allow the whole day to see everything

From the Tourist Information Centre make for the front of the Guildhall and go diagonally left across the Market Place. Use the pedestrian crossing to reach Market Walk. The route is now briefly through a shopping centre before reaching the River Avon.

Ⓐ Turn left over the river and follow the walkway beside the water to Salisbury's parish church. Turn right here and follow Bridge

Salisbury Cathedral was started in 1220 and completed about 1280, though the 404ft (123m) spire wasn't added until the 14th century. The Cloister and Chapter House, which includes a medieval frieze and an original 1215 **Magna Carta**, date back to the time when work on the cathedral was finished. Salisbury Cathedral is the only ecclesiastical building in England to be built in the same Early English style and it remains a permanent monument to the skill of its builders.

**PUBLIC TRANSPORT** Regular bus services to many parts of Wiltshire, train services to Waterloo
**REFRESHMENTS** Plenty of pubs, coffee shops, cafés and restaurants in the city
**PUBLIC TOILETS** Different locations
**ORDNANCE SURVEY MAPS** Explorer 130 (Salisbury & Stonehenge) and Landranger 184 (Salisbury & The Plain). A good street map of Salisbury is also recommended

Street into Fisherton Street, passing the United Reformed Church and the former General Infirmary on the left. Cross Summer Lock Approach and by the postbox is a blue plaque marking the site of the Arts Theatre and Salisbury Playhouse – 1953-76.

**B** Turn left into Water Lane, walk alongside a terrace of striking houses and then swing right at Mill Road. Turn left opposite Harcourt Terrace into Queen Elizabeth Gardens. Follow the path, avoid the first bridge and cross over at the second. Turn immediately right and there are good views of the

cathedral spire along this stretch. Follow the path beside the river to the next four-span road bridge and turn right into Crane Street.

**C** Walk along to the junction with High Street and turn right. On reaching Choristers Green veer right by the telephone box, passing Mompesson House. This National Trust property, open to the public, is a classic example of Queen Anne architecture. Skirt the green and pass the Regimental Museum, which illustrates the story of the county infantry regiments of Berkshire and Wiltshire since 1743.

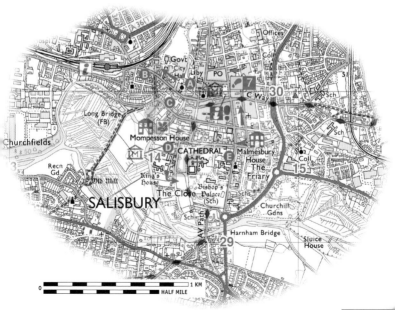

**D** Continue to the Salisbury and South Wiltshire Museum, where there are award-winning displays of archaeology and various Turner watercolours, and turn left just a few paces beyond it. Swing left again alongside the

Of all Britain's great literary figures, it is **Thomas Hardy** who is most closely associated with Salisbury. He loved the city and his two sisters trained as teachers here. 'The Close of Salisbury under the full moon on a windless night is as beautiful a scene as any I know in England,' he wrote. Salisbury was the inspiration for fictional Melchester which appears in some of his books, including *Jude the Obscure*. In the story Jude worked as a stonemason on the cathedral.

cathedral and then head diagonally right across the Close to reach Malmesbury House. Look out for the 1993 memorial to three Protestant Martyrs who burned at the stake in Salisbury in 1556.

**E** Turn left at St Ann's Gate and walk along Catherine Street to the junction with Milford Street. Turn left, pass the historic Odeon cinema building on the left, then swing right almost opposite, crossing Fish Row where it meets Butcher Row. Cut through to the Market Place, back to the start of the walk. ●

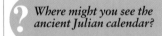
*Where might you see the ancient Julian calendar?*

*The Avon flows serenely through Salisbury*

● Historic church ● canal towpath ● television location ● disused railways

# *Around Wootton Rivers*

**START** Wootton Rivers
**DISTANCE** 3 miles (4.8km)
**TIME** 1¾ hours
**PARKING** Village car park
if not in use
**ROUTE FEATURES** Canal
towpath, farm lane,
stretch of country road,
bridleway and field path.
Some gentle climbing;
bridleways can be muddy

**8**

*The Kennet and Avon Canal runs east-west along the southern boundary of the Savernake Forest and here you will find some of Wiltshire's prettiest countryside. Beginning in the picturesque village of Wootton Rivers, the walk follows the towpath east towards Burbage before leaving the waterway and exploring a gently undulating landscape dotted with trees and criss-crossed by paths and tracks.*

From the car park turn right and walk along to the entrance to St Andrew's Church. The church lies back from the street in a secluded spot reached by a long, enclosed path. On leaving it, return to the road and turn right towards the Kennet and Avon Canal, passing the entrance to Manor Farm.

Ⓐ Cross the waterway via the carriage bridge (number 107), pass

> **❓ Where in Wootton Rivers are you likely to find the words 'Glory be to God'?**

Heathy Close Lock and walk along to the next bridge (106). Cross the road here, passing a sizeable house with tile-hung elevations on the right and a farm on the left, and continue on the towpath to Brimslade Lock, part of the Wootton Rivers flight which was restored in the early 1970s.

Ⓑ Keep ahead beside the canal to reach the next bridge (105) and leave the towpath here. Cross the waterway and follow the lane to merge with an access road to Brimslade Farm. Go straight ahead

**PUBLIC TRANSPORT** Bus services to Marlborough
**REFRESHMENTS** The Royal Oak at Wootton Rivers
**ORDNANCE SURVEY MAPS** Explorer 157 (Marlborough & Savernake Forest),
Landrangers 173 (Swindon & Devizes) and 174 (Newbury & Wantage)

*The Royal Oak at Wootton Rivers*

up the hill, passing a path on the left. Follow the straight road through open farmland and, on reaching the junction, turn right.

**C** Go up the hill and look for a bridleway on the left immediately before the remains of two disused railways. One was a branch line serving Marlborough College. Extra trains were laid on for special events and other occasions during term time. Services operated until the 1960s. Stay on the woodland path and the scene remains largely unchanged for some time.

Eventually, you pass a wide opening into a field on the left. Just beyond it is a path junction. Turn left here and follow the path as it descends to two gateways – one on the left and one on the right.

The lock at Wootton Rivers and this stretch of the Kennet and Avon Canal appeared some years ago in the television series ***The River*** starring **David Essex**. The story was set on the Thames, though it was decided to use the canal at Wootton Rivers as the river was considered too busy for filming.

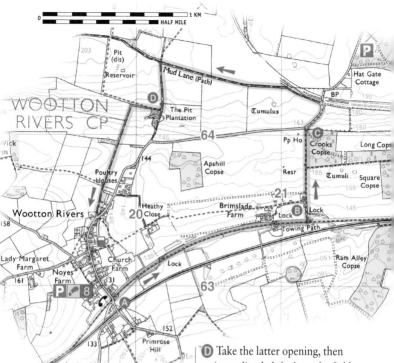

The design of the **church clock** at Wootton Rivers dates back to 1911 and is the work of the amusingly named **Jack Spratt**, an eccentric countryman and amateur clockmaker. To commemorate the coronation of George V, Wootton Rivers decided to provide the church with a clock, though there was no money to pay for it. Spratt came to the rescue and offered to make the clock for nothing, using bits of scrap iron, steel, brass and lead.

**D** Take the latter opening, then go immediately left along the field boundary and round to the right in the corner, passing alongside trees. Elderberries can be seen in season in the hedgerow here. Make for a wide opening and a prominent waymark in the boundary, turn left and drop down between high hedges and trees. Farther on, the houses of Wootton Rivers edge into view. Head for the road, keep right here and walk through the village, passing the 19th century Wesleyan chapel and the Royal Oak.

# 9 *To the edge of the Plain*

*A lengthy ascent from the village of Market Lavington brings you to the edge of Salisbury Plain. If artillery fire is going on, then you won't be able to venture out on to the Plain. But this doesn't affect the route of the walk, which heads west along the scenic northern perimeter of Salisbury Plain.*

**START** Market Lavington
**DISTANCE** 4 miles (6.4km)
**TIME** 1¾ hours
**PARKING** Market Place in Market Lavington
**ROUTE FEATURES** Quite a steep climb out of Market Lavington to the Wessex Ridgeway. Gentle descent across country back to the village

From the Market Place in the centre of Market Lavington turn right and walk along High Street. Pass over a crossroads and continue to the church where you will find the entrance to the village museum at the back. Retrace your steps back to the crossroads **A**.

Turn right into White Street and follow the road out of the village, climbing quite steeply towards Salisbury Plain. Farther up you get a stunning view back down into Market Lavington and over the surrounding countryside. Farther on is a large sign on the right – 'warning to public – danger from

*Market Lavington church*

**PUBLIC TRANSPORT** Bus services to Devizes, Westbury and Trowbridge
**REFRESHMENTS** Pubs in Market Lavington
**ORDNANCE SURVEY MAPS** Explorer 130 (Salisbury & Stonehenge) & Landranger 184 (Salisbury & The Plain)

unexploded shell and mortar bombs'. Continue on the road to Lavington vedette, or sentry box, at the top and turn right to join the Wessex Ridgeway 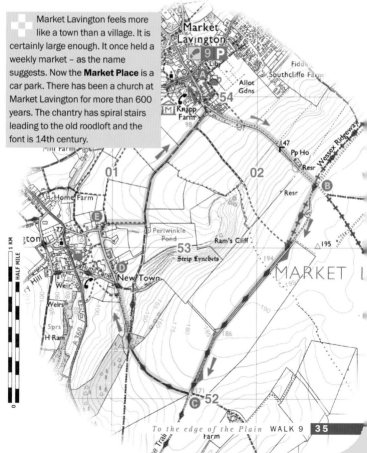.

Walk along the lane, passing a track on the left and a footpath on the right, and continue on the Ridgeway. Avoid a red flag and a track on the right and keep to the

**?** *Where are you likely to see the figure of a dragon in Market Lavington?*

road as it curves to the left. Walk along to a track crossroads and turn right by two bylaws signs – one for Larkhill Artillery Ranges and the other Salisbury Plain military lands .

Market Lavington feels more like a town than a village. It is certainly large enough. It once held a weekly market – as the name suggests. Now the **Market Place** is a car park. There has been a church at Market Lavington for more than 600 years. The chantry has spiral stairs leading to the old roodloft and the font is 14th century.

Follow the track with deep furrows in places and farther down it curves gently to the right, descending through woodland. Pass Stibb Hill House on the left, followed by a picturesque cottage and Rutts Lane a little farther on Ⓓ.

Don't take the lane but keep right here, passing Russell Cottage and Ramscliff. Make for a sign for Stibb Hill. Where the road bends sharp left, turn right and pass the wrought-iron-gated entrance to a house – number 25. Follow the track for about 30 yds (27m) and then turn right to join a narrow path briefly running through vegetation to a flight of steps Ⓔ.

Keep right at the field edge and skirt the pasture to reach a track in the next corner. Turn left here and

When you think of **Salisbury Plain**, the picture that springs to mind is one of an undulating chalk plateau, a hostile, austere landscape with strong evidence of military activity and a tangible air of ancient mystery. The Plain and the whole of North Wessex were once the most heavily populated areas in the country, inhabited by the people of the late Stone Age and Bronze Age. Salisbury Plain is now one of the least populated areas in Britain.

head for Market Lavington. Eventually you reach a cottage; turn left here and keep left at the road just beyond it. There is a sign here for Mount Pleasant Yard. In front of you the road forks – keep right and follow White Street back to the centre of Market Lavington. Turn right and return to the Market Place. ●

*The edge of Salisbury Plain – connected with the Army since 1897*

# The Shears and Collingbourne Wood

*Squirrels may well scamper across your path on this isolated walk through Collingbourne Wood, but you are not likely to see many other signs of life. Once you are clear of Collingbourne Ducis and the pub, the countryside becomes acutely still and silent – perfect for those who want to escape the hurly-burly of the modern world.*

**START** The Shears pub to the east of Collingbourne Ducis
**DISTANCE** 4½ miles (7.2km)
**TIME** 2 hours
**PARKING** Permission has been given to use the car park at The Shears
**ROUTE FEATURES** Largely isolated and very quiet woodland paths and tracks to the east of Collingbourne Ducis. Undemanding climbing

**10**

From the car park turn left and follow the 'no through road'. Pass several pairs of houses and keep ahead. Note a byway sign and a bridleway sign and continue ahead for about 60 yds (55m) to a fork.

**A** Veer right here, follow the byway and begin a moderate climb with good views to the left, down to a dry, remote valley. Keep climbing with hedge and bushes on the right and a fence on the left. Pass a gate on the left with a sign

for a nature conservation area. Avoid a bridleway on the right and continue on the higher ground, passing between lines of trees and carpets of bracken.

**The Shears** is a well-known landmark in this part of Wiltshire and a former coaching inn. The thatched 16th century pub used to be a shearing shed for sheep bound for market at Weyhill. The original building has been extended at the back to provide hotel accommodation.

**PUBLIC TRANSPORT** Bus servces between Salisbury and Swindon
**REFRESHMENTS** The Shears
**ORDNANCE SURVEY MAPS** Explorer 131 (Romsey & Andover) and Landranger 184 (Salisbury & The Plain)

**B** Pass a bridleway on the left and remain on the woodland byway. The surface can be quite rutted and furrowed on this stretch. With glimpses of fields between the trees, keep going and now the path skirts the edge of extensive Collingbourne Wood, managed by Forest Enterprise. Continue ahead for some time, keeping the trees on your left and pasture on the right.

**C** Keep ahead at the next junction, with Blackmore Lane on the right and a bridleway on the left leading into the woods. Continue ahead, maintaining the same direction along a clear, wide track running along Cowcommon Bottom. Over to the right is extensive beech woodland with trees as far as the eye can see.

**D** Take the first bridleway on the left, which is Water Lane, and follow the straight track as it runs through mixed woodland. Pass a cross track and at length the bridleway curves a little to the left. There is a gradual pull through the woodland before you reach a prominent crossroads. Keep ahead with the track curving right now. Pass a track on the left leading to Whittle Copse and when the route sweeps right again, you can see a bridleway coming in to merge from the left. Avoid it and continue.

*The Shears near Collingbourne Ducis*

**E** Turn sharp left beyond the trees, just after a sign for Collingbourne Wood. This is White Lane. Drop down the wide track and keep power lines parallel. Pass a bridleway on the left and continue on the byway alongside beech trees. Avoid a track on the right at the end of the woodland and continue for a short distance between fields.

**F** Turn left just before a steep hill to join a bridleway, keeping fencing on the left. The track curves to the right and immediately to the left of it are grassy gallops. Beyond the trees, continue between pastures and field slopes and make for a gate ahead. Beyond it you retrace your steps back to the Shears. ●

**Collingbourne Ducis** was once held by the Duchy of Lancaster and during the 13th century it belonged to the family of William de Valence, who also held Swindon. For so long the parish of Collingbourne Ducis, including Cadley and Sunton, was considered too small and insignificant to be of any practical use and so it tended to be bypassed by the world – quite literally. It was the railway era and the modern road system that eventually put the village on the map.

*You will see plenty of trees with pointed oval leaves and veins protruding at the edges. What is the species?*

# 11

# *Around the Chutes*

**START** Upper Chute
**DISTANCE** 4½miles (7.2km)
**TIME** 2 hours
**PARKING** Room to park by bus stop in Upper Chute
**ROUTE FEATURES** Mixture of fields, parkland and woodland. Gently undulating with some undemanding climbing

*Pheasants might suddenly burst out of the undergrowth on this delightfully rural walk in Wiltshire's well-wooded border country with Hampshire. This area was once covered with huge tracts of forest and evidence of this still exists today. The Chute Causeway, part of the route, offers a fascinating insight into Roman road building.*

From the parking area turn left towards Chute Causeway. Pass St Nicolas Church and continue along the road round a sharp left bend. About 50 yds (46m) beyond the speed derestriction signs, turn right to join a bridleway.

> **?** *The six church bells at St Nicolas, Upper Chute, were transferred from a church in a forest in 1976. From which forest did they come?*

**A** Descend between hedges and fences and look for the spire of St Nicolas on the right. Follow the path between trees and cross over

*St Nicolas Church at Upper Chute*

**PUBLIC TRANSPORT** Bus services to Andover
**REFRESHMENTS** The Cross Keys in Upper Chute and The Hatchet, Lower Chute
**ORDNANCE SURVEY MAPS** Explorer 131 (Romsey & Andover) and Landranger 185 (Winchester & Basingstoke)

at the next road, continuing on the bridleway. There are glimpses of fields between the trees and bushes. Go down a slope and avoid a bridleway running off to the right. Continue ahead up a gentle slope and swing left at the end of a line of beech trees.

**B** Follow Breach Lane as it twists and winds between trees, climbing gently to reach the road at last. Turn right and follow Chute Causeway, cutting between fields and woodland. This was originally a Roman road linking Winchester and Mildenhall. The lane curves

**Conholt House** is a 19th-century building of grey brick. It was here, just before the turn of the century, that excavations revealed a six-ft wide terrace set with 12-16 in of flints. Some of these looked burnt, indicating how the Romans straightened their roads. By lighting fires at either end of the semi-circular section of the causeway they could line up the plumes of smoke and thus reposition the road.

gently to the right and a barn is seen along here, also on the right. Approach a 'Give Way' sign, with the entrance to Conholt House opposite, and turn right at the junction to a footpath and stile.

*Pretty cottages at Lower Chute*

**C** Go diagonally down the field through Conholt Park, keep to the left of some barns ahead and make for a stile. Follow the path across the next pasture to the next stile and then walk ahead along a grassy track running between fields. Pass over a cross track, descending gently to a waymark. Keep ahead in a rectangular, tree-lined field which tapers. Go almost to the far end and look for a stile and gate in the right-hand boundary, concealed among the trees.

**D** Follow the straight, woodland path and merge with a drive. Pass some barns and stables and a row of cottages and then turn right at the road. Keep left at the junction and pass a variety of picturesque cottages as you walk through Lower Chute. The road curves to the right by a bus stop and telephone box to reach the village war memorial.

**E** Keep right here, pass the Hatchet Inn, veer left at the junction towards Biddesden and head up the slope to a footpath and stile on the right. Follow the path as it skirts gardens, then bends right by some holly trees. Keep ahead on the enclosed path, cutting between fields, and when you eventually break cover from the trees, go forward on a grassy path between fields. Make for the road, turn left and return to the Upper Chute.

*The Hatchet at Lower Chute*

*Peaceful border country*

Chute and **Chute Forest** date back to Norman times and it is thought that the original meaning of Chute is wood or forest. At that time settlements here would have been very small and basic, with just a few cottages occupied by local charcoal burners. Deforestation began in 1632, during the reign of Charles I, who split the area among various nobles. The result of this is still clearly seen today in the pattern of small communities dotted about the area.

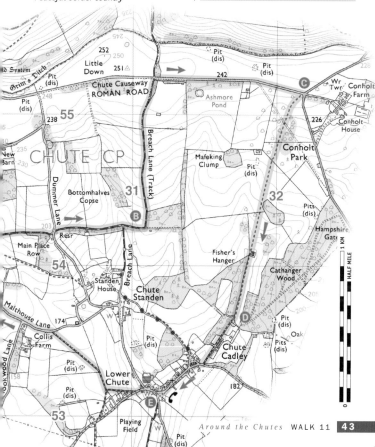

*Around the Chutes* WALK 11 **43**

# 12 *Up above Upavon*

**START** Upavon
**DISTANCE** 4¼ miles (7.2km)
**TIME** 2 hours
**PARKING** Spaces in the village centre
**ROUTE FEATURES** Some paths can be overgrown in places during the summer

*The scenery on this walk is undoubtedly some of the finest anywhere within the boundaries of Wiltshire. Soon after leaving Upavon, you are crossing exposed downland country with stunning views towards the Vale of Pewsey and beyond. During the latter stages, the route explores fertile meadows at the head of the Avon valley.*

With the Ship on your left and the Antelope on your right walk along the main street and turn left in the centre of Upavon, following the A342 Andover road. Keep the parish church and the parish reading room on the left and walk along to a right-hand bend by The Pottery Ⓐ.

Don't take the bend; instead, go straight on, following a footpath

**? What was the Reading Room in Upavon built to commemorate?**

between houses. Soon it becomes a sunken path climbing steadily between trees and banks of vegetation. On this stretch there are glimpses of a magnificent open landscape. Break cover from the trees and bushes and keep ahead on the open ground. Over to the right is the outline of RAF Upavon Ⓑ.

Keep to the left of Upavon golf club, its fairways and greens clearly visible here. Follow the path to the club's north-eastern boundary and descend gently to a track. Turn left here Ⓒ.

**PUBLIC TRANSPORT** Bus services between Salisbury and Swindon
**REFRESHMENTS** The Ship and the Antelope at Upavon
**PUBLIC TOILETS** Upavon
**ORDNANCE SURVEY MAPS** Explorer 130 (Salisbury & Stonehenge), Landrangers 173 (Swindon & Devizes) and 184 (Salisbury & The Plain)

Look to the horizon here and you should see the distant outline of the White Horse, near Alton Barnes. The horse was first carved into the chalk in 1785 and then re-cut in 1937 to mark the coronation of George VI. At this stage of the walk you are more than 500 ft (152m) above sea level. Follow the chalk and grassy track and when it swings right to a 'no thoroughfare – private road' sign, continue ahead on the track.

Pass alongside lines of trees which tend to obscure the view in places. Begin a gradual descent, pass beside belts of woodland on the right and, on a fine day, you might easily spot gliders swooping silently overhead. Make for a T-junction with woodland beyond **D**.

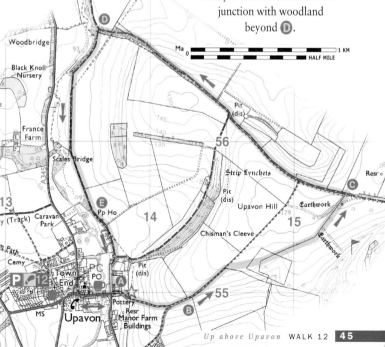

*Views of the Vale of Pewsey*

Turn left here and keep the trees on your right. The sound of traffic is quite audible along here as the path runs close to the A345 road. Cut between hedges and keep parallel to power lines as you begin the final leg of the walk, heading back to Upavon. This is a long, straight section with the River Avon edging into view over to the right **E**.

Merge with a track on the outskirts of the village, pass some old corrugated barns and look for Upavon church across the pastures. On reaching a bridleway sign and another barn, keep ahead and soon the track graduates to a tarmac lane. Pass a row of houses on the left and at the road turn right and return to the village centre. ●

Until around the beginning of the 19th century, there was a busy market at **Upavon**. The meeting point of two important routes also helped to bring trade to the village, and to establish Upavon as a vital and prosperous community between the towns of Andover, Marlborough and Devizes. Not surprisingly, the **old market square** is still the focal point of the village. As well as the restored church with its castellated tower and octagonal Norman font, there are many picturesque buildings in Upavon worth a closer look.

# Downton and Trafalgar Park

**13**

*A varied and very enjoyable walk which starts by discovering Downton's fascinating architectural heritage. From the village the route heads north to a private estate and the remains of a family chapel associated with a familiar name. The walk returns to Downton along a pretty stretch of the Avon.*

**START** Downton
**DISTANCE** 4½miles (7.2km)
**TIME** 2 hours
**PARKING** Spaces in the centre of Downton. Suggested area: in the vicinity of the White Horse at the western end of the village
**ROUTE FEATURES** Quiet road out of Downton and then peaceful tracks to reach Trafalgar Park and the Avon, return to the village along the Avon Valley Path

Keep your back to the White Horse, turn right and walk through Downton. Cross the Avon and keep ahead to the turning to the church. Veer left here and make for the lychgate. Keep right and follow the path beside the library to Barford Lane.

Ⓐ Turn left and head north out of Downton, passing the cemetery and the Catholic Church of the Good Shepherd and Our Blessed Lady Queen of Angels. Keep ahead between pastures and hedgerows and, just before the road bends sharp right, swing left to follow a rough rutted track across the fields. Pass over an intersection of tracks and continue ahead. At length you reach a lodge set against trees.

Downton's origins date back to about 1205 when Peter des Roches, Bishop of Winchester, created a new town to the west of the river. When it became a borough, the burgesses paid their rents in cash rather than holding land against feudal labour and produce. For many years Downton prospered as a centre for industry and commerce. **Lace** became a cottage industry in the area and **handmade paper** was produced at Downton until the end of the Fist World War.

**PUBLIC TRANSPORT** Bus services between Salisbury and Ringwood
**REFRESHMENTS** Pubs in Downton
**ORDNANCE SURVEY MAPS** Explorer 130 (Salisbury & Stonehenge) and Landranger 184 (Salisbury & The Plain)

**B** Go through the gate and turn left. Pass the Nelson chapel on the right and follow the concrete track as it curves left down towards the Avon. On reaching the water, turn right, by a mill cottage, and take the waterside path across a sluice and weir. Follow the clear path across marshes and between reedbeds. Cross several more footbridges and keep ahead over the meadows towards some houses. As you approach them, veer left by clumps of trees in the middle of the pasture and make for a galvanised gate by some semi-detached houses.

> **?** Members of a famous family are buried in the chapel grounds near Trafalgar House. Who are they?

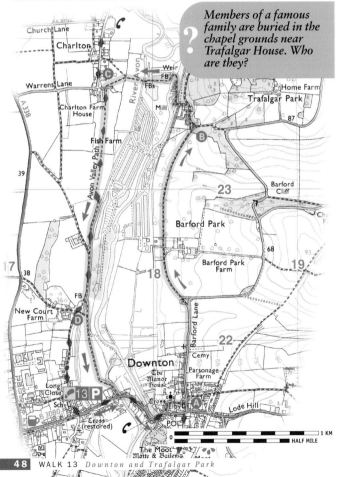

**C** Cross two stiles with a track in between and take the path ahead across the field. Follow it over several stiles to reach a concrete track. Go straight on, keeping to the track until it curves towards a large house and some outbuildings.

**D** Veer left over a footbridge, then swing right, following the track in a southerly direction towards Downton. The river lies over to your left. As you approach the village, the path runs close by the Avon to pass through a kissing-gate. On reaching the road bridge, turn right and walk back to the parking area by the White Horse. ●

Almost halfway round the walk is a redundant chapel associated with Britain's greatest seafaring hero. Near to it is **Trafalgar House**, built in the 18th century. The Trafalgar Park estate was later acquired by the Treasury and given to the descendants of **Admiral Viscount Nelson**, in recognition of his services. The house was later occupied by his brother, the 1st Earl Nelson. This redundant place of worship, rebuilt in 1677 and dedicated for use by the Roman Catholic faith in 1914, became the Nelson family's private chapel.

*The Avon snaking through south Wiltshire*

● National Trust land ● 17th-century folly ● wildlife ● remote downland

**14** *The Pepperbox and Privett Farm*

*Drive along the busy A36 and you are unlikely to notice the Pepperbox folly on the nearby downland slopes, but make for the car park and you can savour this isolated eccentricity. The walk, which starts here, explores exceptionally remote downland country where there are few signs of civilisation.*

**START** The Pepperbox off the A36 between Salisbury and Southampton

**DISTANCE** 4 miles (6.4km)

**TIME** 2 hours

**PARKING** Free National Trust car park at The Pepperbox

**ROUTE FEATURES** The Pepperbox and surrounding slopes, remote woodland paths and downland tracks to the south of the A36

From the car park follow the access track to the A36 and *cross the road with extreme caution*. Take the byway opposite and follow it through a tunnel of trees. Avoid a turning on the left and, on reaching open fields, take the left fork.

**A** Follow the rutted track and farther on you reach a radio mast and a covered reservoir. Continue ahead through woodland and merge with another track coming in from the right. Keep left here, then swing right after a few paces as you approach Privett Farm.

**B**. Pass through the trees and glorious downland views open up to your right now. When the track curves to the left at a fork, keep right and continue in a southerly direction across this wild, open landscape. The track runs through several strips of woodland before reaching a major junction. Ahead are open fields. Turn left here and walk along the track, keeping a large field to your left and woodland on the right. Farther on the track becomes enclosed and, on the left, is an opening into the trees. Avoid it and keep ahead to a right bend.

**PUBLIC TRANSPORT** Bus service between Salisbury and Southampton

**REFRESHMENTS** Pubs in nearby Redlynch, Woodfalls and Whiteparish

**ORDNANCE SURVEY MAPS** Explorer 131 (Romsey & Andover) and Landranger 184 (Salisbury & The Plain)

Have a look at the **artwork** on the information panel by The Pepperbox. It was created by the pupils of All Saints School, Whiteparish. New Forest ponies graze the grassland slopes here in the winter months and more than 100 different kinds of moth have been seen in recent times. Black cap and white throat are among the feathered visitors here, and in winter redwings and fieldfares feed on the berries.

**C** Leave the track at this point by turning left and skirting the field. Dense woodland lies to your left. Look for a gate and opening in the trees about 60 yds (55m) before you reach the first corner. Follow the path into the woodland and after a few paces you reach a fork.

**D** Keep right here and continue between thick scrub, trees and clearings. On reaching a track, keep left and follow it as it sweeps left. Look for a waymarked path on the right, running into the trees and follow it deep into the woodland. Occasional waymarks guide you through the trees. The wood gradually narrows to a strip so that fields are clearly seen either side of the path. Avoid a stile on the right, pass a quarry and eventually emerge from the trees.

**E** Keep ahead with the field boundary on your left, passing light woodland. Curve to the left and keep the A36 over to your right. Make for a gap in the top

*Isolated country near Pepperbox Hill*

corner of the field and follow the enclosed path to the track which formed the initial stage of the walk. Turn right and retrace your steps to the A36. Cross it *with care* and return to the car park.

The Pepperbox is a well-known folly built by Giles Eyre in 1606 in order to overlook neighbouring **Longford Castle**. Regarded as one of the country's earliest follies and otherwise known as **Eyre's Folly**, the Pepperbox is hexagonal in shape with a pyramidal roof. All the windows have been blocked up. The whole site was sold to the National Trust in three lots – the hill with its plants and wildlife, the woods and, finally, the folly.

**?** *Name one of the many grassland flowers that grow on Pepperbox Hill.*

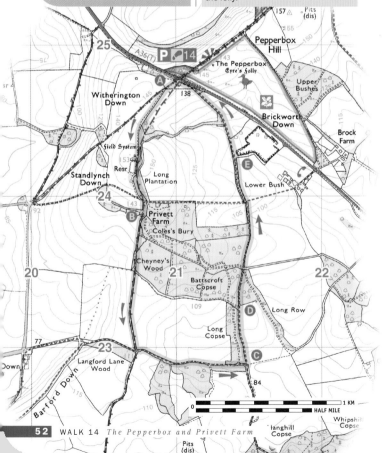

# *Broad Chalke and the Ox Drove*

**15**

**START** Broad Chalke
**DISTANCE** 4½ miles (7.2km)
**TIME** 2½ hours
**PARKING** Free car park for church and village hall
**ROUTE FEATURES** Gradual climb from Broad Chalke to the Ox Drove, dramatic descent over Knighton Hill to the banks of the Ebble

*From Broad Chalke this magnificent scenic walk climbs gradually between chalk grassland, dry valleys and hidden folds flowing off the main track. From the Ox Drove there are superb views to the south and from Knighton Hill Farm the vistas over the Ebble valley are stunning. The last leg flirts with the river.*

From the car park cut through the churchyard, keeping to the right of the church. Make for the lychgate and exit to the road opposite the bus stop, village school and war memorial.

Ⓐ Turn left and then swing right at the left bend, signposted Martin and Blandford. Walk along to the junction and go straight over to follow a stony track. This is Church Bottom. On the right is Field House. Go up the slope and pass a stile and footpath on the left.

Ⓑ Keep ahead along Church Bottom, with woodland on the left.

Pass a barn and now the track begins a steady pull. There are occasional distant views as you climb into the hills. Either side of the track are lines of trees and thick hedgerows. In places, overhanging boughs provide shelter from the sun on a warm day. Farther up, the track climbs steeply to reach a gate on the right. This is Middleton Down.

Ⓒ Continue on the track to a T-junction. This is the Ox Drove, an ancient trade and livestock route linked to the Roman Road from Old Sarum to Dorchester. Opposite is a stunning view of

**PUBLIC TRANSPORT** Bus services between Salisbury and Shaftesbury
**REFRESHMENTS** The Queen's Head in Broad Chalke
**ORDNANCE SURVEY MAPS** Explorer 130 (Salisbury & Stonehenge) and Landranger 184 (Salisbury & The Plain)

Hampshire's south-west corner stretching to the New Forest and the Dorset border. Turn left here and follow the track to a junction with a tarmac lane. Swing left by a storage tank and keep the hedge on the left. Blackberries grow in profusion in the hedgerows here in season. Away to the east are magnificent vistas. Continue to a mast and some farm outbuildings. This is Knighton Hill Farm.

**?** *What do the buildings of Knighton Hill Farm and Knighton Manor have in common?*

**D** Follow the tarmac lane round to the right, then swing left by a barn to join a stony track running round the side of the farm buildings. Keep the mast over to the left and go straight on when you reach the edge of a field, keeping to the right-hand boundary. Look for a gap in the hedge after about 120 yds (109m) and maintain the same direction in the neighbouring field, heading down to a stile in the trees. Below is the lovely Ebble valley.

**E** Descend the steep slope, then

*Broad Chalke church where Cecil Beaton is buried*

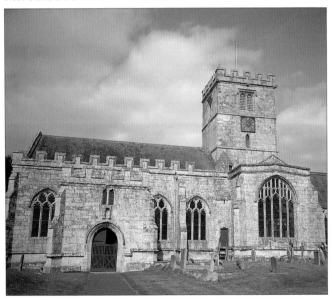

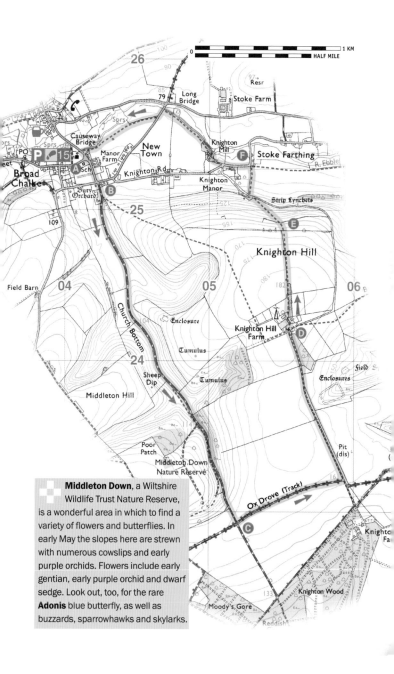

**Middleton Down**, a Wiltshire Wildlife Trust Nature Reserve, is a wonderful area in which to find a variety of flowers and butterflies. In early May the slopes here are strewn with numerous cowslips and early purple orchids. Flowers include early gentian, early purple orchid and dwarf sedge. Look out, too, for the rare **Adonis** blue butterfly, as well as buzzards, sparrowhawks and skylarks.

head diagonally left down the medieval, sunken path to a stile under some trees. A flight of steps takes you down to the road where you cross into a field. Skirt it to a stile and gate by a bungalow. Turn left here and walk along to Knighton Mill.

🅕 Follow the path through the grounds, keeping to the right of the buildings. Cross the stile immediately before the gate and skirt the pasture alongside the Ebble. Make for a stile leading out to the road and turn left. Swing right after about 50 yds (46m) to join a footpath. Cross the field, keeping in line with a row of four trees and passing to the right of a small sewage plant. Make for two stiles to the right of a bungalow and follow the path down some steps to the road. Turn right and return to the car park. ●

That great Wiltshireman and diarist **John Aubrey** was churchwarden at Broad Chalke and wrote affectionately of the village and the Ebble. 'There are no better trouts (two feet long) in the Kingdom of England than here,' he said. He adds that he introduced crayfish into the river though they didn't survive. Aubrey also wrote of the church bells: 'one of the tuneablest rings in Wiltshire'. **Cecil Beaton**, who lived nearby and is buried in the churchyard, donated sums of money towards the church's upkeep in the late 1950s and early 60s.

*Magnificent views of the Ebble valley*

# Nunton and the River Ebble

**16**

**START** Nunton
**DISTANCE** 4 miles (6.4km)
**TIME** 2 hours
**PARKING** Layby near the Radnor Arms in the centre of Nunton
**ROUTE FEATURES** Pleasant paths and farmland in the Ebble valley

*This delightful walk traces the course of the tranquil Ebble close to where it meets the Avon. Beyond Nunton the route follows the river in a westerly direction, crossing fertile watermeadows to reach the picturesque village of Odstock, with its rebuilt 19th century church, including a pulpit bearing the initials of Elizabeth I, set apart from the rest of the community.*

With your back to the layby turn left and follow the road as it curves left. On reaching the A338, turn left, cross the River Ebble and turn left just past the bus stop, following a road used as a public path.

Ⓐ Follow the concrete lane, passing a pair of semi-detached houses and some derelict farm outbuildings and stables. This is Longford Farm. Some of the buildings have been converted into offices and workshops. Continue on a stony track, passing meadows over on the left. Pass another pair of cottages and join an enclosed path running between sycamore trees. Keep fields on the right farther on and eventually you reach the road.

Ⓑ Turn right for a few paces, then left by a gate into a field. Follow the enclosed path before skirting a field. Just before the boundary hedge begins to curve right, turn left through an opening to a stile. Don't cross it. Instead, turn right and keep the field edge on your left. Look for a green lane running off to the left.

---

**PUBLIC TRANSPORT** Buses to Poole, Ringwood, Woodfalls and Salisbury. Some services stop on the A338 while others go through the centre of Nunton
**REFRESHMENTS** The Radnor Arms at Nunton and the Yew Tree at Odstock
**ORDNANCE SURVEY MAPS** Explorer 130 (Salisbury & Stonehenge) and Landranger 184 (Salisbury & The Plain)

Originally Nunton and neighbouring Bodenham were part of the same parish. They were also closely associated with the **Longford Castle Estate**, which crops up in Walk 14, and whose family once owned much of the area. The pub in Nunton takes its name from the Radnor family who still retain the family seat. The village church is mainly Victorian and the 18th-century manor house was built by a successful merchant from Salisbury.

**C** Pass under pylon lines and eventually you reach a track on the right leading to a farm. Avoid it and continue for a few paces to a stile on the left. Follow the wide path through the pastures and cross two footbridges on the far side. On reaching a field, turn left and pass under pylon lines again. Look for the houses of Odstock and make for a stile leading out to the road on a bend.

**D** Walk ahead and turn right at a crossroads. Pass the Yew Tree pub and turn left opposite Shepherds Close. Cross two stiles and then a third to the right of farm outbuildings. Follow the path

between fields, look for Odstock church over to the left and head for a fourth stile. Keep left in the field and make for two galvanised gates.

**E** Turn left at the road, pass trees and a row of houses and when the road bends left, go straight on along a concrete track. Draw level with some farm outbuildings and go through two gates on the left. Walk down the field, keeping to the right edge, and look for a gate in the boundary. Join a woodland

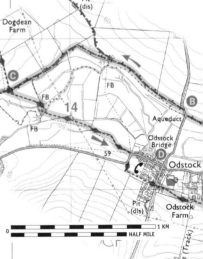

path leading to the road and keep ahead, passing St Andrew's Church before reaching the layby in Nunton where the walk started. ●

*The pretty village of Odstock*

**?** *Where might you see Salisbury's Cathedral spire on this walk?*

In the south-east corner of Odstock churchyard lies the grave of **Joshua Scamp**, a gypsy who was mistakenly hanged for horse stealing at the beginning of the 19th century. Scamp became something of a martyr and each year his supporters gathered around his grave on the anniversary of his death. One day the rector decided to put a stop to this tradition by locking the church door. The gypsies put a curse on anyone foolish enough to try to lock the door and, fearing the consequences, the rector threw the key into the river.

# 17 Pewsey and the Giant's Grave

*This magnificent, bracing walk combines the gentle farming country of the Vale of Pewsey with the spectacular high ground of Martinsell Hill. From the Giant's Grave, a much-loved beauty spot, the views over Wiltshire are truly breathtaking. The route begins and ends on the towpath of the popular Kennet and Avon Canal.*

**START** Pewsey Wharf

**DISTANCE** 5½ miles (8.8km)

**TIME** 2½ hours

**PARKING** Free car park at Pewsey Wharf – maximum stay 4 hours

**ROUTE FEATURES** Pleasant stretches of canal and a steep climb to the Giant's Grave, rewarded with wonderful views over much of the county

Keep to the left of the shop and café and follow the towpath, heading east. Along here are pleasant views over fields and distant downland. Pass under a bridge (113), which marks the return point for the walk, and continue on the towpath Ⓐ.

Completed in 1810, the 87-mile (139m) Kennet and Avon Canal took 16 years to build. The final bill was in the region of £1 million. With 104 locks and many other awesome engineering features, the canal is regarded as a jewel of 18th and 19th century engineering. It was built to provide a direct trade link between London and Bristol, thus avoiding the treacherous south coast route.

The canal eventually became redundant thanks to the nationalisation of Britain's railway network in the late 1940s. But the waterway's armies of supporters were determined not to let it die and, after years of restoration work, the Kennet and Avon was eventually reopened by the Queen at Devizes in 1990.

**PUBLIC TRANSPORT** Bus services between Swindon and Salisbury
**REFRESHMENTS** Café, shop and pub at Pewsey Wharf
**ORDNANCE SURVEY MAPS** Explorer 157 (Marlborough & Savernake Forest) and Landranger 173 (Swindon & Devizes)

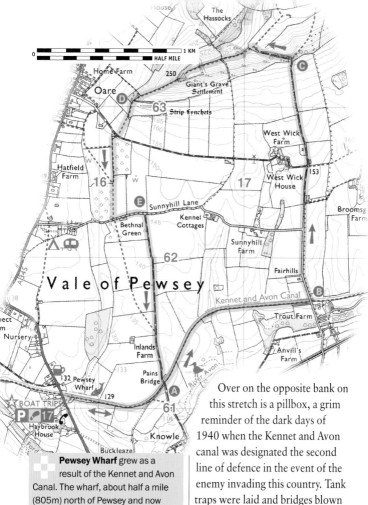

0    1 KM
HALF MILE

The Hassocks
House
250
Home Farm
Oare **D**
**63** Strip Lynchets
Giant's Grave
Settlement
West Wick
Farm
West Wick
House
153
Broomsg
Farm
Hatfield
Farm
**16**
**E** Sunnyhill Lane
Kennel
Cottages
Bethnal
Green
Sunnyhill
Farm
Fairhills
**62**
**Vale of Pewsey**
Kennet and Avon Canal
**B**
Trout Farm
pect
rm
Nursery
Inlands
Farm
Pains
Bridge
**A**
Anvill's
Farm
River Avon
132 Pewsey
Wharf
129
BOAT TRIPS
**P** **17**
Haybrook
House
Knowle
Buckleaze

**Pewsey Wharf** grew as a
result of the Kennet and Avon
Canal. The wharf, about half a mile
(805m) north of Pewsey and now
consisting of a shop and café, was
where canal cargo was loaded and
unloaded in the Kennet and Avon's
heyday. Unusually, during the
Napoleonic Wars, French POWs built
this stretch of the canal and were
summoned to eat at the pub across
the road by a French horn – hence
its name.

Over on the opposite bank on
this stretch is a pillbox, a grim
reminder of the dark days of
1940 when the Kennet and Avon
canal was designated the second
line of defence in the event of the
enemy invading this country. Tank
traps were laid and bridges blown
up but it is unlikely this would have
deterred invasion forces.

Pass the Vera Jean's nature reserve
and keep along the towpath,
completing a lengthy section
before you reach a stile in the right-
hand boundary. Cut through

undergrowth and vegetation to the road and turn left, crossing the canal at this point ⒷB.

**?** *How many different plant species are to be found in the Vera Jean's nature reserve?*

Follow the straight lane between fields, heading towards the escarpment. Pass two pairs of semi-detached cottages and keep on the 'no through road' which is also a waymarked bridle path. Follow an avenue of trees and, when the lane bends left to a farm, go straight on along the concrete track. A house is seen on the left. Keep ahead as the surface underfoot becomes rough and grassy. Soon the track narrows to a path with fields seen to the left.

Make for a gate and swing left at the fork just beyond it ⒸC. Climb steeply through woodland and when you emerge from the tree cover go through a gate to reach a junction after about 30 yds (28m). Keep left to a gate and stile and then walk ahead over the high ground with spectacular views in all directions. To the south lies the

*Pewsey Wharf – popular with wildlife*

*The Giant's Grave, renowned for an amusing legend*

Vale of Pewsey, described by the writer William Cobbett as 'my land of promise'. Cross the Giant's Grave, following the grassy path alongside fencing. Look into the field on the right and you will see a triangulation pillar, originally used by Ordnance Survey to mark an exact height established by surveying instruments. These days the concrete markers are redundant, superseded by advanced satellite technology. Descend the slope, quite steeply at one point, and make for the bottom corner of the field.

**D** Cross a stile and keep left in the field. Follow the path down to the bottom boundary and go through a gate, out to a track. Cross over and continue in the field, keeping to the right boundary. Make for the far corner and turn left at the road. Pass a bungalow and walk along to a sign for Inlands Farm and a bridleway sign for Pewsey.

**E** Follow the track and when it sweeps to the right to Inlands Farm, continue ahead to the canal, cross over and swing left, down to the towpath. Turn left here and retrace your steps back to Pewsey Wharf. ●

The wonderfully named **Giant's Grave** is one of the county's most cherished landmarks. Rising to 822 ft (250m), the summit of **Martinsell Hill** is chiefly associated with a charming legend which claims that anyone who runs along this unchambered long barrow seven times will wake the sleeping giant.

# 18 *Great Bedwyn and Crofton*

*From Great Bedwyn this very attractive walk cuts through the extensive mixed woodland of Bedwyn Brail and Wilton Brail, eventually joining the Kennet and Avon Canal near Crofton. The return leg offers walking beside the unspoilt canal.*

**START** Great Bedwyn

**DISTANCE** 5½ miles (8.8km)

**TIME** 2½ hours

**PARKING** Space to park in the vicinity of the station

**ROUTE FEATURES** Extensive woodland walking and canal towpath. Muddy in places

---

Leave the car park, head for the junction and cross the railway line and the Kennet and Avon Canal. The church tower can be seen on the right. Turn right at the site of the old Bedwyn wharf – coal would once have been transported here from the Somersetshire Coal Canal. Follow the towpath, quite possibly passing an assortment of moored narrowboats, and the church of St Mary the Virgin can be seen across the water.

Ⓐ At the next bridge, just before the lock, turn left through a gate and head up the field slope to a line of mature trees and a fence on the right. Head for the next corner and here you will find a path running off into a belt of woodland on the left. Avoid this and continue ahead by skirting the field and keeping the thick hedge and trees on the right. Make for the field corner and head for the woodland, soon reaching a grassy clearing.

Ⓑ Swing over to the right to join a broad grassy path. Pass over a junction of tracks and paths and continue ahead, signposted 'Windmill'. Follow the obvious track through the trees until you

---

**PUBLIC TRANSPORT** Bus services to Hungerford and Marlborough, train services to Hungerford, Newbury, Reading and Paddington

**REFRESHMENTS** The Cross Keys and the Three Tuns at Great Bedwyn

**ORDNANCE SURVEY MAPS** Explorer 157 (Marlborough & Savernake Forest) and Landranger 174 (Newbury & Wantage)

reach a sign for Wilton Brail. Turn right and follow the grassy woodland ride which is seen undulating ahead. Descend to a squeeze stile and go straight on across a tree-fringed field towards the next section of the path.

**C** Cross a road and continue ahead between the trees of Wilton Brail. Go up the slope between the trees and descend towards the edge of the field. Veer over to the left and keep going through the woodland, passing some

solid oak trees along the way. The path is waymarked in places with white arrows on the trunks.

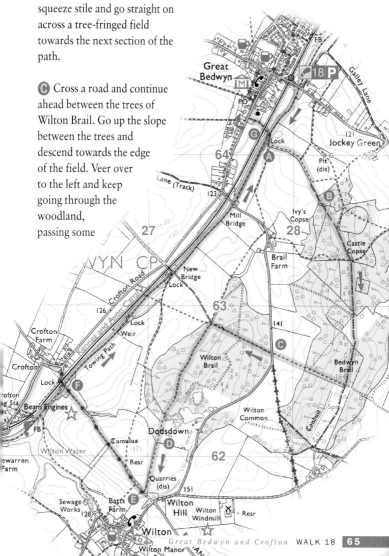

*Canal and church at Great Bedwyn*

**D** Make for the woodland edge and over to the right at this point is Tottenham House, ancestral home of the Ailesburyfamily. Also seen from here is Wilton Windmill, the oldest working windmill in Wessex. Originally built in 1821, it was restored in the 1960s and is sometimes open to the public. Make for a stile in the boundary hedge and keep ahead on the next section of path. Go down the field, pass under power lines and turn right at a track.

**E** This is the route of an old Roman road. Go up the track and the buildings of Wilton can be seen down below. Ahead is the outline of Crofton Pumping Station, seen against the rolling downland slopes. Follow the track between the trees and tall hedges and on reaching the Kennet and Avon Canal you have a choice.

**F** *To visit Crofton, cross the canal and the railway and then follow the lane to the pumping station. Recross the railway and the canal at*

The name 'Bedwyn' is believed to come from the Wiltshire dialect word 'bedwine' or 'bedwind', a term used to describe the wild clematis which is native to the county. The 11th century church of **St Mary the Virgin** includes an effigy of Jane Seymour's father, John. The Seymour family lived in nearby Savernake Forest.

*this point, have a look at Wilton Water and walk back along the towpath.* The main walk now follows the towpath back towards Great Bedwyn. En route is an isolated single-storey building beside the towpath. Pass several bridges and gradually the buildings of the village loom into view.

Ⓖ As you begin to draw level with the church, cross the canal at the footbridge, pass over the Kennet and go through two gates with the railway in between. Follow the path towards the church and make for the main door. On leaving the building, turn right, walk along the street and head back towards the station.   ●

**?** Where, other than in the churchyard, are you likely to see gravestones?

*Crofton Pumping Station*

# 19 Great Wishford to Grovely Wood

**START** Great Wishford

**DISTANCE** 5½ miles (8.8km)

**TIME** 2 hours

**PARKING** Spaces in South Street, near the village stores

**ROUTE FEATURES** Long gradual pull into Grovely Wood from Great Wishford along a downland track. Lengthy sections of path and track within the wood. Winding road through a dry valley to finish

*Tailor-made for those who want to get away from it all, this walk takes you to the heart of Grovely Wood, which is managed for forestry and wildlife and perfect for exploring on foot. Several public rights-of-way cross the forest, and there also various permissive bridleways opened voluntarily by the estate.*

With your back to the church, walk down South Street, keeping Great Wishford village stores and post office on the right. Keep left at the next main junction by Grovely Cottages. Turn right after a few paces to pass beneath the railway line.

**Ⓐ** Follow the obvious bridleway up the slope between fields, climbing steadily with impressive

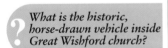

*What is the historic, horse-drawn vehicle inside Great Wishford church?*

Grovely Wood

**PUBLIC TRANSPORT** Bus services to Salisbury, Shrewton, Devizes, Calne and Chippenham

**REFRESHMENTS** The Royal Oak at Great Wishford

**ORDNANCE SURVEY MAPS** Explorer 130 (Salisbury & Stonehenge) and Landranger 184 Salisbury & The Plain

views over woodland and chalk downland. Keep on the track as it makes for woodland and pass a map of the area and a sign welcoming walkers.

Continue between trees and carpets of bracken and climb quite steeply at one point. Pass over a cross track and soon you reach a major junction with a triangular patch of grass.

**B** Turn right here and follow a broad avenue of beech trees. There are glimpses of fields and open downland along this stretch. At length the track sweeps right just beyond a barrier. Don't

In the wall outside Great Wishford church are what are known as the **bread stones**. These tablets indicate the price of a gallon of bread from the Napoleonic Wars onwards. The French blockaded this country at the start of the 19th century and consequently prices rose. Great Wishford was badly hit with villagers paying 8d (3.3p) more for bread than other communities. To reassure residents his prices were genuine, the local baker recorded them in stone in the churchyard wall and the tradition has been maintained ever since.

follow the track; instead, go straight on along a path threading its way through the trees.

*Great Wishford's historic church of St Giles*

*Remote downland near Grovely Wood*

**C** On reaching a tarmac lane turn sharp right, following the Monarch's Way through the woodland. This long-distance trail follows Charles II's escape route after the Battle of Worcester in 1651. Pass another triangular junction and avoid a permissive bridleway on the left. Descend gently and farther down the tarmac surface gives way to stones. This is Grovely Road.

**D** Pass a small parking area on the right and, emerging from the trees, walk ahead through a remote dry valley. On the left at length is a barn. Continue along Grovely Road and eventually a bridge carrying the local railway edges into view as you approach the end of the walk.

**E** Pass a little cemetery on the left and walk under the railway to reach the Royal Oak. Cross a staggered junction and continue through Great Wishford. Turn right just before the church and Great Wishford Church of England School and right again into South Street, back to the start of the walk. ●

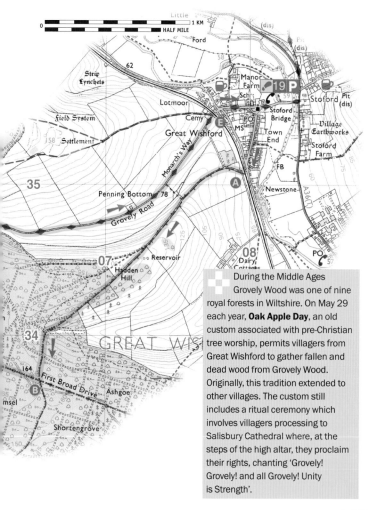

During the Middle Ages Grovely Wood was one of nine royal forests in Wiltshire. On May 29 each year, **Oak Apple Day**, an old custom associated with pre-Christian tree worship, permits villagers from Great Wishford to gather fallen and dead wood from Grovely Wood. Originally, this tradition extended to other villages. The custom still includes a ritual ceremony which involves villagers processing to Salisbury Cathedral where, at the steps of the high altar, they proclaim their rights, chanting 'Grovely! Grovely! and all Grovely! Unity is Strength'.

# 20 Around the Fonthills

*Explore some of the prettiest countryside in south-west Wiltshire on this scenic walk around Fonthill Bishop and Fonthill Gifford, originally built as estate villages, and through Fonthill Park. The route begins at Fonthill Bishop, then cuts across pleasant open farmland to reach Berwick St Leonard. Beyond Fonthill Gifford the walk passes a large lake in the park, where there are teasing glimpses of the water through the trees.*

**START** Fonthill Bishop
**DISTANCE** 4 miles (6.4km)
**TIME** 2 hours
**PARKING** Spaces near the church at Fonthill Bishop
**ROUTE FEATURES** Monarch's Way to Berwick St Leonard, undulating paths and bridleways around Fonthill Gifford, very attractive waterside path beside Fonthill Lake which can get wet and muddy

🖉 Enter the churchyard and follow the path, keeping to the left of the church. Go through a kissing-gate at the far end and continue ahead along the field boundary. Make for a stile and keep ahead in the next field, walking towards Berwick St Leonard.

Ⓐ On reaching a gate, go forward to join a lane, passing some estate cottages on the left. After only a few paces cross the stile on the right and go diagonally across the field towards the church. Cross a tarmac drive and enter the churchyard via a kissing-gate.

*Fonthill Lake*

---

**PUBLIC TRANSPORT** Bus services to Salisbury and Bourton
**REFRESHMENTS** River Barn in Fonthill Bishop and the Beckford Arms at Fonthill Gifford
**ORDNANCE SURVEY MAPS** Explorer 143 (Warminster & Trowbridge) and Landranger 184 (Salisbury & The Plain)

**B** Pass through the gate to the right of the church and swing left to join a drive leading down to the B3089 road. Turn left, then right after about 120 yds (109m) at a bridleway sign. Head south along the field boundary and when you reach a wood, go through a gate and right at the fork. Plunge deeper into the woodland, cross over a path (to the left is a 'private' sign) and descend steeply alongside a wall. Follow the path round to the right, join a track and pass alongside estate cottages.

> **?** *Who maintains the church at Berwick St Leonard?*

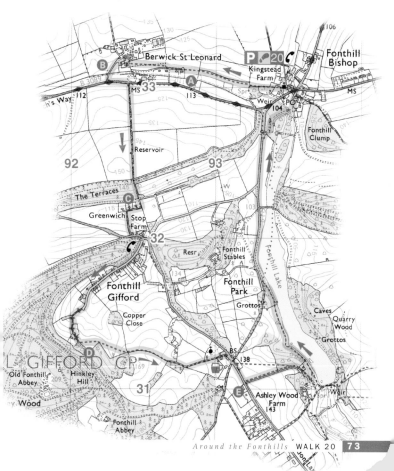

Within the Fonthill estate lies a beautiful lake which was used as a location in the summer of 2000 during the filming of the Joanne Harris novel *Chocolat*. The film stars Judi Dench and Juliette Binoche among others. During filming a mock galleon was intentionally blown up on the lake and various fake features were added to the natural surroundings. Nearby is a splendid arched gateway, a noted feature of the estate, attributed to **Inigo Jones**.

**C** Sweep left to the road and keep left here. Take the first right turning – Stop Street – and pass rows of estate houses and thatched cottages. Climb gradually through Fonthill Gifford and into rolling countryside beyond it. Pass several houses and then turn left at a footpath sign.

**D** Cross the undulating pasture, with Fonthill Gifford seen to the left, and pass into the next field. Go forward to a stile and galvanised gate and join a track to the road. On the left is Holy Trinity Church. Turn right, pass the pub and keep ahead at the junction. Pass the village sign and turn left at a footpath sign. Less than a mile (1.6km) to the west are the remains of Fonthill Abbey.

*Ornate gateway at Fonthill Bishop*

*Fonthill Bishop church occupies a sheltered position*

**E** Follow the track down to a pair of gates and an adjoining gate for pedestrians and, as you approach a second pair of gates, turn sharp left and follow the path beside Fonthill Lake. Keep ahead on the path to the road and turn right. Pass through the elegant park, where the Marquis of Westminster built a Scottish baronial-style mansion, and approach a striking archway. Keep right at the fork just beyond it and return to Fonthill Bishop. ●

**Fonthill Abbey** was built in the late 18th century by William Beckford and described by Pevsner as 'his great Gothic folly'. The Abbey tower was intended to be as high as St Paul's Cathedral. Beckford worked at great speed, employing 500 men to work day and night and keeping fires going to stop plaster and cement freezing. In 1823 he abandoned the place and moved to Bath, his ambitious plans proving too great. Several years later the Abbey collapsed.

# Further Information

## Walking Safety

Always take with you both warm and waterproof clothing and sufficient food and drink. Wear suitable footwear, i.e. strong walking boots or shoes that give a good grip over stony ground, on slippery slopes and in muddy conditions. Try to obtain a local weather forecast and bear it in mind before you start. Do not be afraid to abandon your proposed route and return to your starting point in the event of a sudden and unexpected deterioration in the weather.

All the walks described in this book will be safe to do, given due care and respect, even during the winter. Indeed, a crisp, fine winter day often provides perfect walking conditions, with firm ground underfoot and a clarity of light unique to that time of the year.

The most difficult hazard likely to be encountered is mud, especially when walking along woodland and field paths, farm tracks and bridleways – the latter in particular can often get churned up by cyclists and horses. In summer, an additional difficulty may be narrow and overgrown paths, particularly along the edges of cultivated fields. Neither should constitute a major problem provided that the appropriate footwear is worn.

## Follow the Country Code

- Enjoy the countryside and respect its life and work
- Guard against all risk of fire
- Take your litter home
- Fasten all gates
- Help to keep all water clean
- Keep your dogs under control
- Protect wildlife, plants and trees
- Keep to public paths across farmland
- Take special care on country roads
- Leave livestock, crops and machinery alone
- Make no unnecessary noise
- Use gates and stiles to cross fences, hedges and walls

(The Countryside Agency)

## Useful Organisations

**Wiltshire County Council**
County Hall,
Bythesea Road, Trowbridge,
Wiltshire, BA14 8JN.
Tel. 01225 713000
Rights of Way: 01225 713038

*Crossing the Avon at Amesbury*

**British Waterways**
The Locks,
Bath Road,
Devizes, Wiltshire
SN10 1HB.
Tel. 01380 722859

**Countryside Agency**
John Dower House,
Crescent Place,
Cheltenham
GL50 3RA.
Tel. 01242 521381

**English Heritage**
23 Savile Row, London
W1X 1AB.
Tel. 0845 3010 007

**Kennet & Avon Canal Trust**
Canal Centre,
Couch Lane,
Devizes,
Wiltshire
SN10 1EB.
Tel. 01380 721279

**National Trust**
Wessex Regional Office:
Eastleigh Court,
Bishopstrow,
Warminster,
Wiltshire
BA12 9HW.
Tel. 01985 843600.

**Ordnance Survey**
Romsey Road,
Maybush,
Southampton
SO16 4GU.
Tel. 08456 05 05 05 (local rate)

**Public Transport**
Traveline 0870 608 2608
or 24-hour national train
information line:
08457 48 49 50
www.pti.org.uk

**Ramblers Association**
2nd floor,
Camelford House,
87-90 Albert Embankment,
London, SE1 7TW.
Tel. 020 7339 8500

**Youth Hostels Association**
Trevelyan House,
Dimple Road,
Matlock,
Derbyshire
DE4 3YH.
Tel. 01629 592600

*Colourful activity on the Kennet and Avon*

*St Ann's Gate, one of Salisbury's ancient gateways*

*Tourist information*
www.kennet.gov.uk
www.salisbury.gov.uk

*Local tourist information centres:*
Bradford-on-Avon: 01225 865797/868722
Devizes: 01380 729408
Avebury: 01672 539425
Amesbury: 01980 622833
Marlborough: 01672 513989
Mere: 01747 861211
Salisbury: 01722 334956

Trowbridge: 01225 777054
Warminster: 01985 218548
Westbury: 01373 827158

*Ordnance Survey Maps*
Explorer Maps 130 (Salisbury & Stonehenge), 131 (Romsey & Andover), 143 (Warminster & Trowbridge), 156 (Chippenham & Bradford-on-Avon) and 157 (Marlborough & Savernake Forest).

## Answers to Questions

**Walk 1:** They are both World Heritage Sites.

**Walk 2:** Trout.

**Walk 3:** 189.

**Walk 4:** It is made of concrete which came from nearby Westbury Cement Works.

**Walk 5:** The stone bridge over the Avon near the start of the walk.

**Walk 6:** A plough. It lends its name to the village pub.

**Walk 7:** On the side of Malmesbury House. In 1752 the reformation of the calendar took place. This Julian calendar, dated 1749, made the year too short, with the accumulated error amounting to 11 days. England adapted the Gregorian or reformed calendar so the next day after September 2, 1752 became September 14.

**Walk 8:** On one of the three faces of the church clock, the words replacing numerals. The other two faces are more traditional.

**Walk 9:** Above the entrance to the Green Dragon pub in the village centre.

**Walk 10:** Beech.

**Walk 11:** Chute Forest.

**Walk 12:** The coronation of George V in 1911.

**Walk 13:** The Nelsons, descendants of Admiral Nelson, appear on various crumbling grave stones.

**Walk 14:** Wild orchid.

**Walk 15:** They are constructed of brick and flint.

**Walk 16:** On the waymarks for local paths.

**Walk 17:** 300.

**Walk 18:** The Bedwyn Stone Museum, a small museum where you will see monumental stone masons at work.

**Walk 19:** The oldest known manual fire engine. The churchwardens bought it in 1728, paying £33 and 3s for it.

**Walk 20:** The Redundant Churches Fund.

*Busy traffic near Bradford-on-Avon*